To Adrienne
So that Saratoga may
always feel he's totally
understood!

Dec 92
Love,
Kay

THE LITTLE
CAT BEHAVIOR
Book

ELIZABETH MARTYN
DAVID TAYLOR
Photography by Jane Burton

DORLING KINDERSLEY, INC.
New York

A DORLING KINDERSLEY BOOK

Project Editor Alison Melvin
Art Editor Lee Griffiths
Managing Editor Krystyna Mayer
Managing Art Editor Derek Coombes
Production Hilary Stephens

First American Edition, 1991
10 9 8 7 6 5 4 3 2 1

Dorling Kindersley, Inc., 232 Madison Avenue
New York, New York 10016

ISBN 1-879431-63-7
Library of Congress Catalog Card Number 91-072736

Reproduced by Colourscan, Singapore
Printed and bound in Hong Kong by Imago

CONTENTS

MYSTIC
Cat

*The cat as a source of
mystery and fascination,
and its psychic and
healing powers in myth
and folklore through
the centuries.*

FANTASY AND FOLKLORE

The cat is well known all over the world as a symbol of luck, fertility, and magic.

In Nordic myths and legends, the goddesses Freya and Frigg were powerful figures with a double-edged influence over love, beauty, and destruction. They rode through the air on a chariot drawn by two giant cats. Outside mythology, strange beliefs about cats are still widespread.

FELINE ORACLES
If your cat washes himself in the early evening, expect a friend to visit before nightfall. To dream about a black cat at Christmas time is a prediction of illness in the year to come. A dream about a playful cat is a warning that friends who may seem true are not to be trusted.

In ancient and medieval times, cats were sacrificed to ensure a good harvest. Children were warned not to walk on the fields of corn in case the huge phantom cat who protected the crop should catch them.

HARVEST LORE
At harvest time if a scythe slipped and a man was cut, a cat was brought to the field to lick the wound and so prevent the loss of the crop. In many parts of rural France, cats were garlanded with flowers and ribbons at the start of the harvest. The Japanese kept statues of cats in their granaries to scare away rats with their magical powers.

Left: A white cat
is a symbol of
good luck
Above: Making a
statue of the Egyptian
goddess Bastet
Right: The cat as a
pagan image is
common in cathedral
architecture

WEDDING SUPERSTITIONS

According to French folklore, a bride who mistreated a cat would go to the church in pouring rain, while a white cat sitting on the doorstep before a wedding was a sign of lasting happiness. In the Netherlands, however, a cat sitting by the door on the wedding day was a bad omen, since this meant that the cat had not been treated with respect, and the bride would treat her husband in the same way. On the other hand, if a cat sneezed near a bride, she would be assured of good luck.

FELINE BAROMETERS

Keep a close eye on your cat's behavior and you may never need to listen to a weather forecast again. The way you interpret the signs depends on where you live. In England, cats are supposed to predict rain by washing behind their ears; in China by winking an eye; in Scotland by rubbing against the legs of a table; and in Denmark by racing up and down the stairs. Scottish cats can predict gales by clawing at the furniture. A cat sleeping curled tightly into a snug ball is telling its owners that cold winter weather is on the way. But a cat who dozes with its legs sprawled out in front of it is predicting a heat wave.

The White Cat

STORM CATS

In the past, a cat was used on ships to whip up strong winds and storms. On a becalmed ship, a cat would often be used in a ceremony, performed on the ship's bridge, to make the wind blow harder. Throwing a cat into the ocean was another sure way of causing a storm, and shipwreckers were thought to have used this method to try and sink treasure-laden ships. According to East European folklore, cats were possessed by demons during thunderstorms and the bolts of lightning were spears thrown down from heaven to exorcise the evil spirits. As a result, cats were often locked out of doors when there was a storm to prevent the house from being hit by lightning.

Left: Fairy-tale cat
Right: Lucky black cat
Below: Cat with its back to a fire predicts frost

BEST OF FORTUNE
~HEALTH AND WEALTH~
MAY YOU HAVE ALL THINGS
YOU WISH YOURSELF

PSYCHIC CATS

Cats have always had strong connections with
witchcraft and the supernatural.

The ancient
Egyptians
believed that
cats could
protect them
from spirits,
and buried cat-
shaped amulets
with their
dead to ward
off any evil.

supernatural
powers and in
league with
the devil.

MAGICAL COMPANIONS

A witch, it
was supposed,
could even
turn herself
into a cat
during unholy
black magic
rituals. With
their highly developed senses,
cats certainly seem to be able
to perceive things that are not
apparent to humans. There are
many well-documented cases of
cats showing great agitation
and then fleeing from buildings
before an earthquake. The most
probable explanation is that
they are very sensitive to slight
shifts in the Earth's magnetic
field and to the build-up of
any static electricity in the air.

DEMON CATS

In Russia, a cat
was put into a
new cradle to drive out wicked
spirits before a baby was
allowed to sleep in it. When
someone died in China, cats
were kept out of the house, in
case they called back the soul
as a zombie. In the Middle
Ages, cats were persecuted
because they were seen as
witches' companions. Cats,
especially black cats, were
often thought to be demons
in disguise, possessed with

Left: A witch predicts the future with the help of her companion
Right: Witch and black cat take flight on a broomstick
Below: 16th-century demon cat

CAT GHOSTS

There are numerous recorded sightings of ghostly felines, including a case in 1892, when a woman who was tending her sick grandfather saw a strange cat that promptly hid itself. The next day her grandfather died, but not before another member of the family had seen a ghostly cat walk around the bedroom, and then disappear into thin air.

HEALING CATS

Cats have long been associated with health, and there are many accounts of their healing powers.

Cats were regarded as sacred by the ancient Egyptians, and were therefore safe from the kind of human cruelty meted out in later centuries. From medieval times different parts of cats' bodies, ranging from the dried liver to the blood and bones, were used to concoct every kind of cure and medicine.

CAT CURES

There were cat-based cures for all manner of complaints, including blindness, skin diseases, unrequited love, and depression. It was even thought that a human could make himself invisible by holding a bone of a black cat under his tongue. Black cats were always in demand among witches, who by rubbing themselves with an ointment made from the cat's fat could supposedly turn into felines and go about their evil business unnoticed.

TALL TAILS

But not all of the medicines required the cat to perish. The tail of a live black cat, stroked across the eye, was said to cure a sty, while the tail of a cat of any color was useful in the treatment of nettle rash and epilepsy. A cat flung after the devil, when the latter visited a graveyard at midnight, would take its owner's warts with it.

Left: Elderly people are often
advised to keep a cat
Above: A mysterious potion
Right: A calming companion

COMFORTING CATS

Owning a cat has proven health
benefits. The survival rate after
a heart attack is higher among
cat owners, and stroking a cat
has a soothing effect and can
even lower blood pressure.

ACTION
Cat

The amazing feline physique: a repertoire of cats leaping, prowling, balancing, and playing with perfect ease.

RUNNING AND JUMPING

Supple body structure enables a cat to leap and
bound with consummate grace.

BORN HUNTER

A cat's body is designed for the all-
important feline skill of hunting.
Cats can creep silently, lowering
their bodies close to the ground and
treading lightly on their paws. If
need be, they can also produce
bursts of high speed, although they
can only keep these up over a
short distance. The bones of the
hind legs are arranged like a
lever mechanism and these,
coupled with strong muscles,
produce the effortless spring
that a cat uses to pounce.
The front claws, which are
kept razor-sharp, and
the sturdy teeth are
used for efficiently
killing prey.

THROUGH THE AIR
*The eyes are fixed on the
intended landing point.*

EFFORTLESS LEAP

Before making a leap, a cat will often spend some time assessing the distance it has to cover, flexing its muscles. The cat needs a firm surface for the take-off. The strong muscles in the hind legs thrust the cat up and into the air. The cat lands with all four feet as close together as possible and the tough paw pads help to absorb the shock of the impact.

ENERGY CONSERVATION

A cat is always prepared to spring into action, chasing any moving object that catches its attention, from a falling leaf to a passing bird. When not racing around, a cat strolls, with a minimum of effort. Some cats, especially older ones, always seem to move at a gentle amble.

IN MIDAIR

Cats can easily jump to several times their height.

CLIMBING AND BALANCING

Cats are as skilled as tightrope walkers when it comes to edging along a narrow ledge or balancing nonchalantly on a tiny perch.

Up Aloft

Cats enjoy looking down on the world, and will go to great lengths to clamber up to inaccessible roosting places for a better view. The ears play an important part in balancing, as they do in humans, and a cat also uses its tail to help it keep its footing. More important than the tail, however, is the back, which is exceptionally flexible. The spine is held together by muscles that enable a cat to twist and weave. The position of the shoulder blades on either side of the rounded chest and the lack of a collarbone mean that a cat can bring its front paws in under its body and tread daintily along the narrowest surface.

Commanding View

On top of a dresser or in a tree, a cat loves to be in the top spot.

Head for Heights

Most cats are very good at climbing up trees, but not nearly as good at coming down again. The reason is that on the way up, the cat uses the strong hind claws to support its weight while it gets a firm grip with the front claws to pull itself up. The front feet can also be twisted around for a better grip. But coming down is harder because the cat cannot get such a secure grip. The front claws are weaker and cannot support the cat's weight for more than a few seconds. Sometimes a cat will try to descend headfirst, or will back down nervously and often rather clumsily. The only alternative is to fall and, although cats usually do land safely, most prefer not to take the risk of injuring themselves.

Branching Out
The tail acts as a useful counterbalance.

PLAYING

Watching your cat at play can be great fun, as it leaps, pats, and pounces. But there's a serious purpose behind the games.

PLAYFUL PRACTICE

When your tiny kitten stalks a ball of yarn or leaps onto a defenseless ping-pong ball, it is obeying a primitive instinct and trying out the skills it would need to feed itself as an adult in the wild. Play is all about hunting and toys are no more than practice prey. That is why a mother cat encourages her kittens to play boisterous games from a very young age.

FELINE TRICKS

The energetic play indulged in by many older cats acts as a safety valve that enables them to let off steam safely. Their natural instinct to hunt is frustrated because their kind owners provide regular meals.

CATNIP TREAT

Any toy scented with catnip will keep your cat amused for hours.

HOME RUNS
Many cats become expert at ball games, and learn to hit home runs, dribble, and score goals just like professional athletes.

TOYS TO ENJOY
Simple toys provide cats with a chance to learn how to move and manipulate objects. Cats are clever at picking up small objects in their teeth. They can also grasp a plaything between their front paws by rising on their back legs, and can bring their hind paws into play if they roll over onto their backs. Even adult cats find it hard to resist the temptation to pat at a small item to see whether they can knock it onto the floor, where it can be pounced on from a great height.

WORLD OF

Cats

*An intriguing
exploration of the
feline senses and cat
communication.*

SIGHT

A cat's eyes are very large in relation to the overall size of its face. This is a typical characteristic of animals that hunt at night.

CELESTIAL CAT

The ancient Egyptians believed that the moon was the eye of an enormous celestial cat and it was a cat's eyes that inspired Cleopatra's eye makeup. The Celts thought that if you gazed into the eyes of a cat you would see into a tiny fairy kingdom.

BURNING BRIGHT

Cats cannot see in the pitch dark, but a vestige of starlight or moonlight is all they need to find their way around. Their eyes are designed to make maximum use of what little light is available. The pupils can expand from vertical slits in bright light to large, black circles when light is limited. A layer of iridescent cells inside the eye reflects light back onto the retina. This is what gives the eerie effect of night shine, when a cat's eyes glow mysteriously in the dark.

ALL AGLOW

Reflective cells send back a ghostly beam of light from a cat's eyes in the dark.

Cats' Eyes

Cats can see better than humans in poor light, but they are not so good at picking out detail.

Color Sense

Biologists agree that cats can see in color, but their eyes do not have a sophisticated mechanism for differentiating between colors. They can probably make out blue, but red would appear as a murky gray, and green and yellow would appear much the same. A genetic fault in some white cats makes them odd-eyed, with one orange eye and the other blue. In these cases, blue eyes are associated with deafness and the cat may have trouble hearing on that side.

So Surprised

Feline eyes come in three basic shapes: slanted, almond-shaped, and round like this cat has.

HEARING

A cat's hearing is acute and is one of the senses it relies on for information about its environment. Every owner knows that a cat can hear the sound of a refrigerator door opening from several streets away.

SONAR DETECTION

Where humans have only six muscles in each ear, cats have 30, enabling them to twist, turn, and flex their ears very accurately to pick up passing sounds. The irregular shape of the outer ear also helps cats to pinpoint an interesting noise precisely. Inside the cat's skull are hollow echo chambers that amplify sounds, making them easier for the cat to identify.

HIGH FIDELITY

Cats can pick up very high-pitched sounds, like the squeaks of tiny prey animals, that cannot be discerned by humans. Even dogs, who can also hear high-frequency noises, do not have such sensitive ears. However, cats start to lose this useful skill at around three years old.

EAR SIGNALS

A cat's ears are an indication of its mood. This cat's ears are pointed forward, showing its friendly interest in what's going on.

WORD POWER
Most cats recognize words such as their name by the tone of voice used, but few understand a wide vocabulary.

SNOWY SILENCE
White cats often suffer from deafness because the gene that gives them their coat color can also cause ear malformation.

BALANCING ACT
The cat's highly sensitive ears are useful not just for listening, but also as a center of balance that help it to perform all sorts of precarious and acrobatic feats.

TOUCH AND SMELL

A cat's body is supremely sensitive to touch, and its quivering nose can pick up the most delectable scents over long distances.

Scent Sensation

When a cat thrusts its face into the breeze, nose aquiver, it is using its highly developed sense of smell. The feline nose is equipped with four times as many scent-detector cells as a human nose. The sense of smell is very important in the cat world. Kittens can identify their mother by her scent, even when they are still deaf and blind. And, because all cats use their scent glands to mark out their territory, smell is a vital indicator of the movements of other cats in the vicinity.

Fussy Eater

Offer a cat any new delicacy and it will take a polite sniff before deciding whether to accept your offering. A cat's nose is exceptionally sensitive to smells containing nitrogen – a sure sign that food is not as fresh as it might be. The Jacobson's organ on the roof of the mouth helps to identify particularly stimulating odors.

On the Trail

Cats use their ultrasensitive noses to gather information about their local surroundings. By giving a good sniff to tree trunks, fence tops, and the like, a cat can tell which of its feline friends and foes have passed by, and how long ago.

LOVING TOUCH

The feline body is touch-sensitive all over, which is why your cat loves to be stroked, or washed by feline companions.

THE CAT'S WHISKERS

Every cat possesses three sets of long hairs that are extremely sensitive to pressure: the whiskers, the eyebrows, and the long hairs between the front paw pads. The whiskers are rigid and wiry and are not sensitive in themselves, but even a slight change in air currents will be detected by the whisker pads.

SUPER SENSORS

Whiskers can be brought forward, to check ahead.

BODY LANGUAGE

Every move your cat makes tells you something about
what he is thinking or the way he is feeling.

S*AYING* H*ELLO*
Cats greet other strange
cats by turning their head
to one side or by raising
their head and drawing it
back. This is usually
done to avoid a fight.

Cats who know each other well
may rub their bodies against
each other. One cat may crouch
and offer its spine for the other
to rub. These are typical
gestures of affection between a
mother cat and her kittens, and
a good way of reinforcing scent.

F*RIEND OR* F*OE?*
A cautious but not unfriendly greeting
which indicates that neither of these two
cats is really looking for a fight.

Territorial Rights

A cat intent on scaring off an intruder looks very ferocious. With ears held back, pupils narrowed, a wide and snarling mouth, and bristling tail, lashing fiercely to and fro, this is an animal to approach with caution. The cat who's on the receiving end of this treatment will look suitably cowed, crouching low in an attempt to look as small as possible and slinking away as soon as there's a chance to escape.

Back Off

The raised hackles and bushed tail are an effective warning to any potential opponent.

Mother Love

Kittens love to snuggle up to their mother's furry body, partly for affection, partly for warmth, and partly because they feel safe surrounded by her familiar scent.

THE MATING GAME

A female cat can produce two litters of kittens a year.
So, unless you can find good homes for all those
adorable kittens, you should have your cat neutered
before you let her go outdoors.

FEELING FRISKY
Although female cats are fertile
from around seven months, it is
better for them not to breed
until they are at least one year
old. Tomcats reach sexual
maturity slightly later,
at between ten and
fourteen months.

ROLL ME OVER
*No mistaking the message here:
a female in heat rolls seductively to
capture the tom's attention.*

COURTSHIP RITUALS

A female cat will only mate with a male who takes her fancy. She may "call" loudly when in heat in order to attract all the eligible local toms, but will reject the advances of unfavored suitors. The male cat has to advance very slowly, making soft sounds and gradually getting close enough to sniff her. The courtship can go on for several hours.

MADE FOR MOTHERHOOD

Most cats enjoy looking after their kittens, and make loving and attentive mothers. The father, if he is around, is unlikely to show much interest in the young. In the few hours after she has given birth, a female cat will even accept the young of other species for mothering. One cat is on record as bringing up a young rabbit and a family of squirrels as if they were her own.

LOVING TOUCH

Neck-nibbling, licking, and other signs of affection are all part of courting behavior.

CAT CHAT

A dictionary of feline sounds to help you have meaningful conversations with your cat.

*P*URRING

🐾 There are many different "levels" of purr, from a chesty sound that can be heard across the room to the gentle, soft purr of a snoozing cat.

🐾 Cats purr to indicate pleasure and contentment, but the sound also has other meanings. A mother cat purrs as she approaches her kittens to reassure them that all is well.

Aggressive Sounds

❦ Hissing and spitting sounds terrify other cats, and are very effective warning signals.

❦ A growl low in the throat is the next stage of aggression.

Chattering

❦ Cats make this strange, teeth-chattering sound when they have spotted a tempting prey. The cat may crouch low and wag its tail as it watches an unsuspecting bird.

Chirping

❦ This pleasant little sound is often used as a greeting. Some cats even use it to converse with their owners.

Safeguarded

Any stranger approaching her litter of kittens will be greeted by a snarl or hiss from this protective mother cat.

Meow

❦ Some cats hardly ever utter a lusty meow, whereas others are very talkative. This sound can be used in many different ways.

Caterwaul

❦ The unattractive sound made by toms out roving at night.

Chatty Cat

"You don't look like a kitten." This little chap tries a puzzled "Meow?" on his new friend.

Cat
ON THE
COUCH

*A fascinating analysis of
feline temperaments to help
you understand your own
cat's character.*

THE SOCIABLE CAT

The beautiful Balinese is known for its fondness for human companionship. This sociable cat will follow you lovingly from room to room and will always want to know exactly where you are and what you are doing.

Bright Eyes
The friendly cat scrutinizes all newcomers with interest: those glorious blue eyes are irresistible.

TRUE TRUST
A true sign of trust: an invitation to tickle her abdomen.

PERSONALITY POINTERS
An affectionate nature coupled with a very playful streak, in kittens and adults alike, make this kind of cat fun to be with.

SOCIABLE BEHAVIOR
A cat who likes to snuggle down on your lap and is never averse to a cuddle. Inquisitive and intelligent, this friendly feline will quickly fit into your daily routine.

CAT MAINTENANCE
Keep your sociable cat happy with lots of attention, and don't leave her alone too often or for too long.

CATERISTICS
Ready to make friends with any new human

Enjoys a good game

Understands every word you say

WHAT'S NEW?
Nothing escapes the sociable cat's keen interest in life.

THE CONTENTED CAT

Another name for this sleepy tabby could be the lazy cat. Lolling in the sun or in front of a warm fire is her idea of bliss and the most strenuous exercise she is likely to take is a short stroll to her dinner bowl. The minute a human lap becomes vacant, this cat will hop onto it and settle down with a contented sigh, happy to stay put for just as long as you'll let her. She's a very soothing pet to have in the house: stroking her is guaranteed to reduce tension.

GETTING COMFY
Every so often the contented cat will roll or stretch, before settling down again.

PERSONALITY POINTERS
Gentle and soft-hearted, this is a cat who seldom complains as long as she's given plenty of food and a warm bed.

I'M WATCHING YOU
Even sleepy cats keep an eye on what's going on around them.

Forty Winks
*This lazy cat would much
rather be curled up by the
fire than outside hunting.*

Contented Behavior
Sometimes the contented
cat might chase a butterfly.
More often, she's sound
asleep and purring.

Cat Maintenance
The first priority is a choice of
cozy snoozing spots, scattered
conveniently around the house
and garden. Second is hours of
uninterrupted time to spend
catnapping. Third comes lots of
human affection.

Cateristics
✦
*Will always wake up for a
stroke or to be told how
beautiful she is*
✦
*Likes to try different
beds now and then*
✦
*Not always as deeply
asleep as she looks*

THE WARRIOR CAT

Meet the warrior cat, a ginger tomcat with a battling nature and a personality that suits the color of his coat. He protects his own territory ferociously and, although he's fond of people, other cats take cover when he's on the prowl.

FIERY FIGHTER
Not all meetings end in fisticuffs. Both cats must want to fight before coming to blows.

CATERISTICS

Old warriors are recognizable by their battle scars

May stay out all night, or longer

An extremely noisy character

PERSONALITY POINTERS
Although this tough character terrorizes the neighborhood males and pursues the female felines, at heart he's a bit of a softie. His owners probably don't realize the mischief he makes, unless he comes home battle-scarred, because he can look very innocent.

Top Cat

The warrior cat will get into fights with other toms over desirable female cats, or if another cat should be foolish enough to stray into his domain.

Warrior Behavior

Frankly, the only way you can improve this cat's behavior is by having him neutered. Tom-cats never lose their aggressive instincts, or their lust for the ladies, although they may become less troublesome as they get older.

Cat Maintenance

It's doing everyone a favor to keep a cat like this indoors at night: other cats will love you for it, not to mention the neighbors who would otherwise be kept awake by his nocturnal caterwauling. If you decide to have him neutered he will lose interest in combat, but may still have an eye for attractive females.

THE CURIOUS CAT

Nothing's safe from the precision paws of the curious cat. This inquisitive feline can open closets, find a way into drawers, inspect the contents of refrigerators – and you'll never know how she managed it. A curious cat will want to investigate the slightest noise or even the tiniest movement spotted out of the corner of her eye.

So Playful

Any unfamiliar object is seized on and turned into a toy by this inventive cat. As long as she can pat it or chase it, she's interested. Her playful antics are always a delight to watch.

CURIOUS BEHAVIOR
Unpredictability is the order of the day with a curious cat about the house. You never know where she'll pop up next: under the covers, in the folds of the newspaper, or hiding behind the chest of drawers.

CAT MAINTENANCE
You'll need patience and a sense of humor to live happily with such a bundle of mischief. Make certain areas out of bounds from day one by keeping doors and drawers firmly shut whenever your cat is looking for a new game.

ROUND EYES
This kitten can't help but look inquisitive with her wide eyes.

PERSONALITY POINTERS
Lively and full of beans, these cats have a wide, alert gaze and never miss a trick.

CATERISTICS

Can't resist the challenge of any closed door

Always turns up where least expected

A mischief-maker who needs supervision

PROWLING PUSS
Stalking, pouncing, and chasing are all part of the fun for a cat who's fascinated by any tiny movement.

THE EXTROVERT CAT

The striking Abyssinian is an extrovert cat who requires a lot of attention and play with his owner as a part of the daily routine. An active cat, he needs plenty of exercise and becomes restless and bored if he is kept cooped up indoors.

PERSONALITY POINTERS
An affectionate and intelligent pet who will learn tricks and games quickly, this cat is happiest when involved in some kind of activity.

EGYPTIAN FEATURES
The Abyssinian is descended from an ancient breed, but its noble features are the result of careful breeding.

COVETABLE COAT
The beautiful ticked markings on the Abyssinian's coat may not develop fully until the cat is at least 18 months old.

CATERISTICS

Should be allowed
some freedom to
roam outside

Easily bored; needs
to be kept amused

Always interested in
what's going on

EXTROVERT BEHAVIOR

There's not an ounce of malice
in this cat, but such a lively
character will wreak havoc
with your furniture and
curtains if he is neglected.

CAT MAINTENANCE

As long as he's kept amused
and has access to a large
garden, this cat will be
perfectly happy.

ROUGH-AND-TUMBLE

Abyssinian kittens can be extremely
boisterous, and many of them never seem to
grow out of their love of kittenish games.

THE TIMID CAT

The Russian Blue is typical of the timid feline that is always happy to fall in with its owner's wishes. Sensitive by nature, it avoids strangers wherever possible, and prefers to stay at home rather than wandering far afield. This quiet cat rarely uses its voice.

PERSONALITY POINTERS
A quiet cat, such as the Russian Blue, is a good pet for the anxious owner who likes to know that puss won't stray far. This cat is perfect for people who live in apartments, as it doesn't mind being confined.

SOLEMN GAZE
This feline spends hours sitting thinking.

TIMID BEHAVIOR
Although shy with people it doesn't know, this charming feline is always eager to please its owner. It makes an obedient and affectionate pet.

CAT MAINTENANCE
Sympathetic owners will be attracted to the contemplative nature of this cat and will share its desire for peace and quiet.

PAMPER ME
This sensitive cat likes to be spoiled now and then with its favorite tempting recipes.

CATERISTICS

Always seeks out
the warmest spots

A peace-lover
who's not interested
in fighting

Perfectly happy to
live indoors

LUCKY CAT

The timid Russian
Blue originated in
Russia, where it is
thought to bring
good fortune to
its owners. Its
elegance and
the softness
of its fur are
second to none.

CAT STARS

How the stars influence your cat's personality.

ARIES
MARCH 21 – APRIL 20

Cats born under this sign never say "meow," but "me, me, me." Whether they want to be fed, petted, or just admired, Arien cats will insist that you stop whatever you are doing and give them your undivided attention. Fortunately, the antics of these cats are always fun to watch.

TAURUS
APRIL 21 – MAY 21

You won't catch a Taurean cat madly rushing around. This sign likes to consider its every move and seldom behaves impulsively. Taureans can be stubborn, and like to stay put until they are ready to move. Strong on determination, these cats get what they want.

GEMINI
MAY 22 – JUNE 21

These cats are often pretty, with delicate features and huge, expressive eyes. Geminian cats are very "talkative" and will make a wide range of sounds to let you know how they are feeling. Unpredictable, they are happy and bright one day, but withdrawn the next.

Cancer
JUNE 22 – JULY 22

Never trifle with a Cancerian cat's emotions. These cats are very sensitive. They will reward your affection by being delightful companions, but they are quick to take offense. Cancerians can't bear to be laughed at or neglected, and need constant reassurance that they are loved.

Leo
JULY 23 – AUGUST 23

If you're not careful, a Leo cat can take over the entire household, demanding specially cooked meals, luxurious bedding, and the most comfortable chair around. In return, these cats will love you devotedly and amuse you with their prima donna behavior.

Virgo
AUGUST 24 – SEPTEMBER 22

Virgoan cats pride themselves on their looks and every last whisker is always spotless. To keep a fastidious Virgo happy, you will need to ensure that both its feeding bowl and bedding are scrupulously clean, otherwise it will turn up its immaculate nose and walk away.

*L*IBRA
SEPTEMBER 23 – OCTOBER 23

Librans have great charm and will quickly win their owner's devotion. This cat will come running to greet you, wind adoringly around your legs, and leap onto your lap the minute you sit down, and, because Librans are so cuddlesome, you won't mind a bit.

*S*CORPIO
OCTOBER 24 – NOVEMBER 22

If you want an intense relationship with your cat, choose a Scorpio. Fiercely devoted, a Scorpio cat will be your faithful friend, but won't sacrifice its own independence. This is a fascinating cat, extremely intelligent, with deep emotions and a strong need for love.

*S*AGITTARIUS
NOVEMBER 23 – DECEMBER 21

A cat stuck in a tree is bound to be a Sagittarian. Cats born under this sign are extremely curious and often get into trouble. Fortunately, their lucky streak usually saves them from harm. They are fun to live with, if you can accept their adventurous spirit.

CAPRICORN
DECEMBER 22 – JANUARY 20

Capricornian cats have a delightful sense of humor and will often make you laugh with their winning ways. These cats dislike any change and will be most upset if you move their bed or interrupt their routine. Home is always best for Capricornian cats.

AQUARIUS
JANUARY 21 – FEBRUARY 18

Don't try to spoil your Aquarian cat. This sign is definitely not cuddly. Only rarely will Aquarians permit you to give them a caress. These are light-footed, inquisitive creatures that dart around like quicksilver, always appearing where you least expect them.

PISCES
FEBRUARY 19 – MARCH 20

Serene and cool, Piscean cats have a mystical quality. They tend to keep themselves apart from human activities, looking on with interest, but not joining in. But they will sense when their owner needs cheering up, and offer affection at the right moment.

CAT WATCHING

What type of personality does your cat have?

1 How would you describe your cat's character?
a Loves a good cuddle.
b Enjoys affection, but very seldom demands it.
c A bundle of energy.
d Distant and self-contained.

2 Which kind of company does your cat prefer?
a Humans, every time.
b Only people she knows well.
c People, cats, dogs, children…
d Her own.

3 What kind of game does your cat like best?
a Any game that you play.
b Chasing her tail – when no one's looking.
c Racing up the curtains.
d No one's ever seen her play.

4 Where does your cat usually spend the night?
a On your pillow, with her face pressed against yours.
b Curled up in her basket.
c Out on the street.
d Ghost-hunting.

5 How does your cat react to other cats?
a Not that interested.
b Runs a mile.
c Curious – not averse to a fight.
d Keeps a good distance.

6 How does your cat treat visitors to the house?
a Leaps onto their lap to greet them in the first five minutes.
b Hides until they've gone.
c Jumps on them from a height.
d Watches them with interest, but won't come near.

7 How and where does your cat like to take her nap?
a Curls up by your side.
b Tucks herself out of sight.
c Soon wakes up, ready for fun.
d Sleeps with one eye open.

8 How skilled a hunter is your cat?
a Prefers to stalk humans.
b Can move very stealthily.
c Will tackle anything – but not always successfully.
d No bird or mouse is safe.

9 What's the best way to persuade your cat to come home in the evening?
a Shout her name very loudly from the back door.
b Call repeatedly in a soft voice.
c Rattle the feeding bowl.
d She'll come when she's ready, and not before then.

10 How chatty is your cat?
a Purrs constantly whenever she is near people.
b Only meows when necessary.
c Very talkative – always has something to say to you.
d Has her own very personal vocabulary that no one else can understand.

YOUR CAT'S PERSONALITY TYPE

MOSTLY As:
Sociable and fond of people, this cat thinks she's human.

MOSTLY Bs:
A shy cat who likes people but is inclined to be timid. Needs encouragement.

MOSTLY Cs:
What an extrovert. You'll never have a dull moment with this cat in the house.

MOSTLY Ds:
This is the cat who walks by herself. Unfathomable, mysterious, and totally fascinating.

I N D E X

Acknowledgments

Key: t=top; b=bottom

All photography by Jane Burton except for:
The Bridgeman Art Library: 11t · E.T. Archive: 12
Mary Evans Picture Library: 15t · Fine Art Photographic Library Ltd: 16
Michael Holford: 17t · The Image Bank: 10
Images Colour Library: 11b, 14, 15b · Dave King: 52, 53
Ann Ronan Picture Library: 13b, 17b

Design Assistance: Patrizio Semproni, Rachel Griffin, Camilla Fox
Additional Picture Research: Diana Morris
Illustrations: Susan Robertson, Stephen Lings, Clive Spong

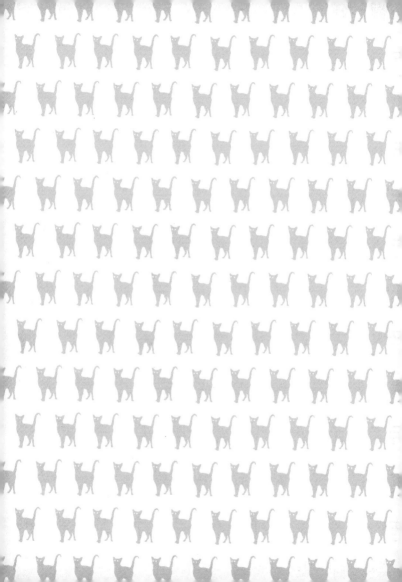